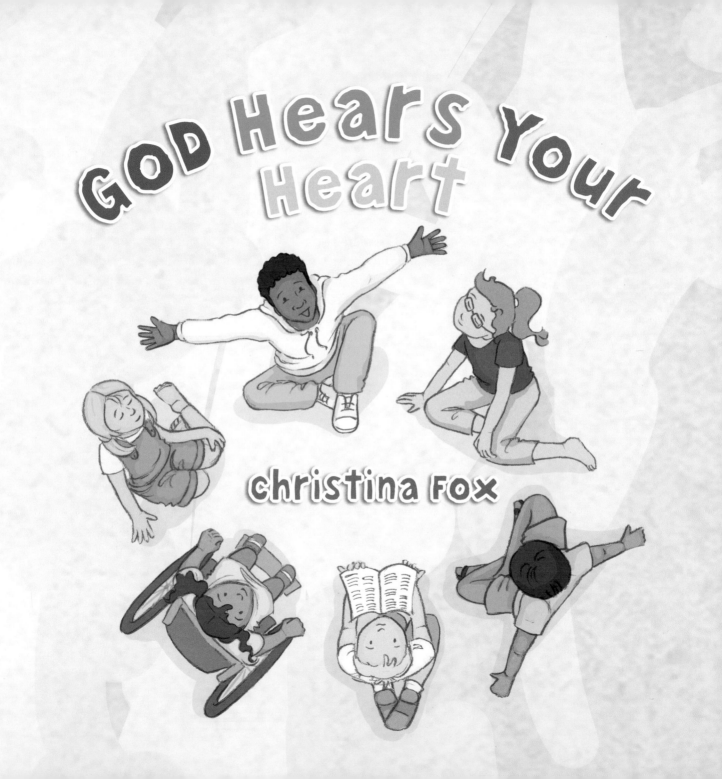

God Hears Your Heart

Christina Fox

God Hears Your Heart is a wonderful resource for children. It accomplishes the difficult task of turning children toward the Lord with their hard and unruly emotions without moralizing or excusing. Especially good on the disappointments every young human struggles to deal with and full of good advice and easy engagement for parents, this book is a must on every child's bookshelf!

J. Alasdair Groves Executive Director of CCEF
(The Christian Counseling and Educational Foundation)
and co-author of *Untangling Emotions*

If emotions are complex for adults (AKA, me!) to understand and respond to appropriately, how much more for children? This is why I'm so glad Christina has given us a helpful tool for guiding our kids through emotions like disappointment, anger, and failure. Best of all, she roots each lesson in biblical truth, particularly in the psalms which give voice to our hearts. I recommend this book to you!

Kristen Wetherell, mom of two, author of *Fight Your Fears*,
and co-author of *Hope When It Hurts*

To my nephew Joseph

God hears
when you pray

Copyright © 2022 Christina Fox
ISBN 978-1-5271-0840-0

Published in 2022
by Christian Focus Publications
Geanies House, Fearn, Ross-shire, IV20 1TW
Scotland, U.K.
www.christianfocus.com

Illustrations by Lisa Flanagan
Cover design by Lisa Flanagan

Printed and bound by Gutenberg, Malta

CONTENTS

1. An Angry Outburst

2. A Disappointing Day

3. A Hard Failure

4. Feeling Guilty

5. A Joy-filled Heart

Dear Parents,

God Hears is a book designed to help you as a parent engage your child/children on the topic of emotions, and more specifically, difficult emotions. It is a follow up book to *Tell God How You Feel,* with a similar format and the same characters (and a few new ones).

We are emotional beings. Created in the image of God, we reflect God; we mirror Him in this world. One of the ways we do that is in our emotions. God feels emotions such as love, joy, peace, jealousy, anger, and sadness (Exod. 34:14, Rom. 1:18, Rom. 5:5, John 11:35). When we feel joy and gladness at the goodness of God, we image Him. When we feel righteous anger at the effects of sin in the world, we reflect God.

But unlike God, our emotions are not holy and perfect. Like all things, sin has impacted our emotions. The impact of the Fall brought on by our first parents' sin is felt far and wide. Bad things happen. People get sick and die and we mourn their loss. People hurt and abuse us. Frightening things happen in the world around us—disasters, pandemics, violence, job loss, divorce, and more. We hurt others with our selfishness. All of these situations are the result of sin and they all produce emotional responses within us. Sometimes we respond in sinful ways to the pains of life. Often, our emotions will cloud the truth, exaggerate the truth, or distort the truth.

That is why developing the spiritual discipline of turning to God's Word to shine the light of truth into our circumstances is so important. *God Hears* helps children learn that God's Word is our source of hope when our emotions take us on a roller coaster ride. When we are hurt, sad, angry, or disappointed, God's Word is the anchor that keeps us secure.

Psalms of Lament:

If you are unfamiliar with the Psalms of Lament, there are a few things you should know to help you as you teach your children about the Psalms. First, the book of Psalms is the Bible's hymn book. The Israelites used the Psalms in their worship the way we sing our hymns and spiritual songs in church on Sunday mornings.

The book of Psalms contains many different types or genres of prose, written by a number of different authors, including David, Moses, and Israel's worship leaders. The Psalms are not organized by type, but as you read them, you can tell that they are different. Some Psalms are praise songs, singing praises to God for his goodness and faithfulness. Some are songs of thanksgiving, thanking God for a specific deliverance. There are also dark Psalms called laments. These are the Psalms where the writer voices difficult and painful emotions. He tells God in vivid and descriptive words and metaphors that he is sad, afraid, or lonely, among other emotions.

The laments have a common pattern. They usually begin with the author describing their circumstances and how they feel about it. The author then asks God to help or to intervene in some way. At the end of the lament, the author often ends with words of praise and worship. It is this pattern we want our children to learn and implement in their own prayers to God.

children and their emotions:

1. Children need to learn to identify their emotions: Children don't automatically know that the tightness in their belly or the pounding of the heart means they are afraid. They need the words to describe it. It's important that we help our children gain a vocabulary for naming their emotions. You can help them by using words that describe emotions. You can describe your own emotions, "We are running late to our appointment and I'm worried we will miss it." "I am feeling frustrated because my computer isn't working today, and I can't get my work done." You can also point out to them when you identify their emotional responses, "You seem worried about your spelling test today." "I see that you are crying. Are you feeling sad because _____?"

2. Children don't always behave the way we expect: A child who is sad might not behave the way an adult does who is sad. Sometimes, increased psychomotor activity, distractedness, whining, and irritability are all indicators that a child is emotionally bothered by something. Emotions like fear, sadness, and loneliness can show up in strange ways. When your child is behaving differently than normal, consider what emotions might be lying beneath that behavior.

3. Emotions are part of what the Bible calls the "heart": The Bible includes our emotions as part of a broader term, called the heart. When we read about the heart in the Bible it includes our thoughts, emotions, will, intention, choices, and beliefs. There is a strong relationship between our beliefs and emotions. What we believe and think shapes our emotions. That's why not everyone has the same emotional response to the same life circumstance. When we train our hearts through reading and studying God's Word, it transforms our thinking, which in turn will

shape our emotions. This is why reading the Psalms helps us when we are going through a trial or difficult season. The Psalms remind us of what is true and in encountering the truth, we find our joy renewed.

4. We also have a body: Not only do we have a heart, but we also have a physical body. Our physical bodies impact our spiritual nature and vice versa. There is a complex relationship between the two. For example, we know how much stress impacts our physical health. When we consider our children's emotional responses, we have to remember this truth. Sometimes physical health problems can impact their emotions. We see this when they are tired or hungry. Medications can cause a change in emotions as well (For example, after a recent surgery, I woke up in the recovery room crying. I later learned it was a common side effect to anesthesia). As parents, we need to keep in mind the impact of our children's physical health on their emotions and seek medical help as needed.

5. Children need to know that emotions themselves aren't bad, it's how we respond to them that can be sinful: It's true, our emotions are not always an accurate indicator of reality. But they do tell us something is wrong. They reveal something in our heart. And while they aren't bad in and of themselves, we can respond to them in sinful ways. Feeling hurt and rejected by peers is a normal response to the unkindness of others, but it's not right to then turn and yell at a sibling. In helping our children learn to lament, they will learn a godly response to their painful emotions. And as they mature (both in age and in spiritual wisdom), you can help your children learn to search their hearts and identify what thoughts, desires, and beliefs might be influencing their emotional responses.

6. Often, the ways we deal with our own emotions will come to the surface in response to our children's emotions. If we are uncomfortable with emotions, if we tend to stuff or hide what we are feeling, it will be difficult to help our children with their emotions. Here's the truth: we can't just tell a child, "Stop being sad" or "Stop being angry." Rather, we need to help direct their emotions to the one who knows and cares about their emotions. We need to help them see that God is their place of safety, their refuge to turn to when life hurts.

7. We all have a natural response to get rid of what hurts us. We all want to hide from difficult or uncomfortable emotions, pretend they aren't there, or cover them up. As adults, we might eat a gallon of ice cream when we are stressed or upset.

We might keep ourselves busy to distract ourselves from the things that bother us. Children might respond differently, but they still have a natural tendency to want to protect themselves from uncomfortable emotions like fear and sadness. Be on the lookout for that. *God Hears* is designed to help children learn to turn to God when they are upset rather than whatever they naturally want to do with their anger, disappointment, or other emotions.

8. An additional accompaniment to learning how to lament, is to help your children learn more about God's character. Consider taking the time to study the names of God and His attributes with your children. Another topic worthy of study with your children is that of God's providence. These truths are ones that the psalmist turned to in his pain and sorrow and it's what our children need to do as well.

Ways to use this book:

1. Simply read it like you would any other picture book with your child. There are discussion questions at the end of each story which will help you engage your children about what they learned.

2. Read a particular story that relates to what your child is going through. If you know your child is dealing with angry feelings about something, read Josh's story and talk to your child about what Josh learned about his anger.

3. Some of the discussion questions are designed for younger elementary children and others are for older elementary children. Use the questions you think are best suited to your own child.

4. The stories chosen for this book are circumstances that most children will face in their childhood. Some children experience more painful and frightening situations than those in this book, such as abuse and severe loss. Even if your child has not experienced the exact circumstance as the child in the story, they still know what it's like to feel anger, disappointment or failure. Use the discussion time to help them think through how they can relate to the emotions in the story, if not the exact scenario.

May this time with your children draw you closer to each other and to the Lord your Refuge.

christina fox

A Note to Kids

from Josh and Mia

"Hi! My name is Josh."

"And I'm Mia."

Josh: "What you are about to read are some stories about our life. We are kids just like you and sometimes, life gets hard. We feel all these things, but don't know what to do with our feelings."

Mia: "Yeah. Like the time I almost missed my best friend's birthday party."

Josh: "Or when I was so mad, I shoved another kid at school."

Mia: "We all have big feelings sometimes and it's hard to know what to do with them. It almost seems like our feelings take over. Josh and I want you to know that we all feel that way sometimes."

Josh: "We also wanted you to know that God cares about what hurts. He cares about how you feel. And He wants to hear from you. He wants you to ask Him to help you when things seem so big and so hard. He wants you to trust Him to help you."

Mia: "So when you read the stories about our big feelings, remember that even if you have not had the same story as ours, you probably know what it's like to feel the way we felt."

Josh: "Thanks for reading, and welcome to our story!"

An Angry Outburst

Josh carried his lunch tray to his class table in the lunchroom. It was pizza day, a favorite among his classmates. As he walked toward his table, he passed his sister Mia, sitting with a group of friends.

Some boys were standing next to Mia and Josh heard them calling her names. He immediately stopped and walked up to the boys.

"What's going on here?" he asked.

Mia sat frozen. Her eyes were large and she seemed afraid. Her friends were quiet, looking down at their food trays.

"Oh, just talking to Miss Know it All here," one of the boys commented. "We're reminding her of what happens to people who think they are better than others. She needs to stop answering so many questions in class or the teacher will start to expect everyone to care so much about stupid stuff like history." He sneered at Mia and the rest of the boys laughed.

Josh felt his face burn and his fists clenched as he watched these boys bully his sister. He stormed up to the ringleader and shoved him backward. As the boy fell, he knocked into the boys behind him and they fell too. Lunch trays clattered onto the floor and food spilled all around. The lunchroom monitor saw it and ran over to the group, calling for assistance from other teachers in the room.

Josh soon found himself in the principal's office, waiting outside her door.

"Josh!" a familiar voice called.

He looked up and saw his mom walking down the hall.

They both looked up at the sound of the door opening and Mia came out of the principal's office.

"What happened? Why did the school call me to come in for a meeting?"

He looked down at his feet on the floor and shrugged. "I don't know," he muttered.

"Mia," her mom said, "what happened?"

Mia looked at Josh and then at her mom and then back at Josh again. She hesitated, opened her mouth to respond, and then the principal came out to see the family gathered there. Mrs. Galloway smiled and remarked, "There was a conflict in the lunchroom today and I wanted to talk to you about it."

Josh and his mom joined the principal in the office, and Josh recounted what had happened. "I was just so mad at what they were saying to Mia!" he exclaimed. "Someone had to stand up to them."

Mrs. Galloway looked at Josh and said, "I heard from Mia what the boys said to her. It was wrong of them to say such things and they will receive a consequence for their actions. We do not tolerate bullying at this school." She paused, directed her gaze at Josh, and continued, "However, it is equally wrong for you to shove the boys."

She continued, "Since we attend the same church, and since I've known you since you were born, I'm going to talk to you now as a fellow church member and not as your principal. Josh, we all feel angry at injustice and we should. When God created the world, He created us to love and serve Him and one another. But because of sin, we don't live as we should. We put ourselves first and are quick to be unkind. There's nothing wrong with feeling angry about what happened to your sister. But God calls us to not sin when we are feeling angry and you did so."

Mrs. Galloway then looked at Josh's mom and told her, "I'd like you to take Josh home for the rest of the day and he is to stay home tomorrow as well. I hope you will talk with him about this, so it doesn't happen again."

Josh's mom stood up and thanked Mrs. Galloway and assured her that she and Josh would talk about it at home.

Once they arrived home, Josh's mom made him a snack and they sat down at the kitchen table to talk. Josh told her how angry he felt when his sister was bullied by the boys at school. "I'm still mad!" he proclaimed.

Mom reminded Josh of the story they recently read during family devotions, the story of David and how his enemies lied about him and chased after him to kill him. "David felt angry too. In fact, he once had an opportunity to kill King Saul, but he didn't do it. He knew it was wrong and instead waited for the Lord to deal with Saul. But what David did do was tell God about his anger." She then read from Psalm 109:

"Be not silent, O God of my praise!
For wicked and deceitful mouths are opened against me,
speaking against me with lying tongues.
They encircle me with words of hate,
and attack me without cause" (vv. 1-3).

"That's like those boys! They attacked Mia without cause," remarked Josh.

"David then asked God to help him and deliver him and he praised and worshiped God," Mom continued. "Josh, when you feel angry, you need to tell God about it. Ask Him to help you. And when you are in a situation like today, you need to ask an adult to intervene. Bullying is wrong and God put adults in your life who have the authority to deal with it. Do you understand?"

"Yes. I'm sorry you had to come get me from school," Josh said.

Mom smiled, gave him a hug, and said, "Let's pray and tell God about what happened today. And then how about we have a cookie while we read more about what happened between David and King Saul?"

Questions for Discussion

1. Have you ever been angry like Josh was in this story?
What happened?

2. Mom and Dad, share a story about a time you felt the same way.

3. Read what Paul says about anger in Ephesians 4:26.
Is it always wrong to be angry?
When is it right to be angry?
What does God want us to do with our anger?

4. Why is it important to tell grown-ups when other
people have been unkind to us?

5. For older children, read Psalm 4 and talk about how
God hears us when we pray to Him.

6. Pray together, helping your child tell God
about angry feelings and asking for His help.

A Disappointing Day

"Mia! Time to get up! You have a big day ahead!"

Mia rolled over and looked at her clock on the nightstand. 8:00. She quickly sat up and remembered that it was Saturday, and she was to meet her best friend for a birthday party.

She got dressed and ready for the day and practically skipped her way to the kitchen for breakfast.

"There you are!" Mom remarked. "I thought you'd never get up," she said with a smile. "Are you ready for your fun day?"

"Yes!" Mia said. "So, you'll drive me out to the farm to meet up with my friends where we'll spend the day riding horses and then we'll have a cookout for Lydia's birthday and then we'll spend the night out under the stars. Lydia says I get to pick which horse I want to ride. Can I have some sugar cubes for the horse? Should I bring an extra blanket for camping out? Oh, I need to make sure I pack Lydia's present. Do you think she'll—"

Mom stopped her. "Slow down, Mia! We have time to get everything sorted before I drive you out to the farm. Now finish your breakfast."

Mom and Mia loaded everything in the back of the car and Mom shut the door. "I think you brought enough for a week," Mom remarked.

Mia laughed. "Well, I just wanted to be prepared."

They got into the car and Mom turned the key to the engine. It made a funny sound but started. They took off down the road. The farm was almost an hour away from their house. As they drove along, Mia and her Mom chatted more about Lydia's birthday party.

All of a sudden, smoke started billowing out of the car's hood and the car made sputtering sounds. Mom pulled over to the side of the road. They were far outside town, surrounded by cow pastures.

"What's wrong with the car?" Mia asked.

"I don't know," Mom said as she tried to get a signal on her phone.

"Dad is in a meeting at church. I'll call him." But she couldn't get through.

"We're going to be late," Mia moaned as she plopped down
on a big rock on the side of the road.

Mom kept trying to make calls,
both to Dad and to a roadside assistance company.

"Mia, I think we'll need to walk a bit until we can get a signal. Otherwise, we won't get any help."

They walked along the road, continuing to try and make phone calls for help.

Eventually, they came upon a farmhouse and Mia's mom decided they ought to knock on the door and ask to use the phone.

An older woman answered with a friendly smile. After Mom explained what happened, she responded, "Of course, come on in and have a seat. I'll bring you the phone."

Mom called the roadside assistance company and they said it would be a while before they could arrive. Mom then called Dad who said he would come as soon as he could.

"Well Mia, it looks like we'll be waiting a while," Mom said.

Mia's eyes started to tear up and she said, "I'll miss everything!"

"I'm sorry, sweetie." Mom hugged Mia. "I know it's disappointing. We will do our very best to get you to the farm for the party."

"I was looking forward to seeing my friends and riding horses all day," Mia moaned.

Mom and Mia sat on the kind woman's front porch and drank lemonade while they waited for news about when the tow truck would arrive.

Mom said, "Mia, life is often disappointing. Do you know why?"

"Because cars break down at the worst possible time?" Mia asked.

Mom smiled. "Well, that's part of it. A big part of it is because we live in a fallen world where things don't work as they should. After Adam and Eve's sin, everything in life was broken. This includes not only our sinful hearts, but also the things we work hard to create, the things we make, and even our plans. It's right to feel disappointed when things don't go as they should. When our plans get interrupted, it's okay to feel sad about it."

"I'm really sad," Mia said fighting back tears and staring down at her lemonade glass.

"God wants to hear from you when you feel that way. He wants you to tell him about your sadness and disappointment," Mom said.

"He does? He cares about me missing the party?" Mia asked in surprise.

"He sure does. Remember what we've been reading in the Psalms? The psalmist told God everything he felt: sadness, anger, fear, loss, guilt, and more. He asked God to help him. He knew God loved him and that only God could help and deliver him."

"Should I tell Him right now?" Mia asked.

"Well, we aren't going anywhere anytime soon," Mom commented.

Mom and Mia sat together on the farmhouse's front porch and prayed to God about their disappointing day. Mia told God how much she had looked forward to attending the party and how sad she was to miss it. She asked God to help her, to bring the tow truck soon, and that she would make it to the party before it was over.

"Thank you for loving me," Mia prayed. "Thank you for hearing me when I pray. In Jesus' name. Amen."

The kind lady brought out some sandwiches for lunch. Mom and Mia played a game of cards and tried to pass the time, when a loud noise made them look up to the road. A huge truck pulled up in front, with their car attached to the back. A man got out and came up to talk to Mom. While they were talking, Dad pulled up in his car.

Mia ran out to Dad, yelling, "You're here!"

He laughed. "I came as quickly as I could. I met the tow truck at the car and put all your things in my car. Let's get you to that party!"

After thanking the kind woman again for her hospitality, Dad, Mom, and Mia piled into Dad's car and headed on their way to the farm.

As they pulled up to the farm, a group of girls came running.

"Mia, where have you been?"

Mia told them everything that happened. Lydia said, "We missed you on our horseback ride. It wasn't as much fun without you."

They went on to tell her about all they had done so far.

"I'm sad I missed it," she said. "Did I miss everything?"

"No. You didn't. We were thinking of going on a short ride on a trail near the house before setting up everything for camping and the cookout," Lydia said.

Mia's face lit up, "Really?" She turned to her Mom and Dad, "Did you hear that?"

"Yes," Mom said with a smile. They helped her put her things in the farmhouse and then waved goodbye. "We'll see you after breakfast tomorrow. Have fun!"

Mia snapped her helmet in place and gave the horse a pat on the neck. "Thank you, Lord, for helping me get here. Thank you for giving me the opportunity to ride with my friends," she whispered as they took off down the trail.

Questions for Discussion

1. Have you ever felt disappointed when something didn't go the way you expected? Talk about what happened.

2. Parents: share about your own disappointments.
(A job you wanted but didn't get. An important event that was cancelled.)

3. Why don't things always work out the way we want them to?
Talk about the impact of the fall of man on everything in life: toys break, events get cancelled, we get sick, people do things that impact our plans, etc.

4. Read Psalm 25:16-18. How does David feel?
What does he ask God to do?

5. For older children, talk about Proverbs 16:9 which says, "The heart of man plans his way, but the LORD establishes his steps." God sometimes changes our plans for us. We don't always know why He does so, but we do know God is good and has good plans for us. When things don't go the way we expect, we trust in God's plan for us.

6. Pray together, telling God about your child's disappointments. Ask God for His help. Pray about God's character and great love for your child.

A Hard Failure

Josh stood in his bedroom looking at the shelf above his bed. It was filled with sport trophies. He had played many sports since he was in preschool, but his favorite was swimming.

He loved the feel of his arms pushing through the water, the sound of muffled cheers from his coaches, and the thrill of popping his head up and seeing his time posted on the board. This season, he was trying out for a travel swim team. It was a big deal. It meant more early morning practices, and not swimming just one season a year, but year-round.

Dad walked by Josh's room, saw him standing there staring, and asked, "What's up?"

Josh turned and said, "Just thinking about the tryouts tomorrow."

"Are you ready?" Dad asked.

"I hope so. I'm worried I won't be fast enough compared to the other kids trying out. What if I don't make it?" Josh responded.

"You've been practicing hard," Dad commented, "I know you'll do your very best."

Dad sat down on Josh's bed. "What would it mean to you if you didn't make it?" He patted the bed next to him and Josh sat down beside him.

"That I'm a lousy athlete. That I'm not the swimmer I think I am ... that, I'm a failure," Josh whispered the final part and heaved a big sigh.

Dad pulled him into a hug and said, "Your value and worth as a person doesn't depend on how you perform at something. Whether you make the team or not, whether you are the best swimmer or not, I love you. Mom loves you. You are important to all of us."

"I know, Dad." Josh rested his head into his dad's side.

Dad turned to him and said, "But even more importantly, you are loved and valued by God. Not because of your swimming abilities, but because He made you. You belong to Him. He loves you. Remember that."

Josh smiled. "I will."

The next morning came fast. Josh finished his breakfast, grabbed his swim bag, and stuffed it with his goggles, towel, and suit.

"Are you guys ready?" he called.

Dad, Mom, and Mia came down the stairs and they all piled into the car. When they arrived at the swim center, the parking lot was nearly full.

Josh signed in and went to the changing room to get ready for his tryout, while his family went to the stands to watch.

Time seemed to stretch long as he waited for his age group to be called. Finally, Josh lined up on the side of the pool. He looked up and down the row at the other boys preparing to dive in. Some he knew from other swim meets. He nodded and smiled at them and then looked down, readying for the start.

"Splash!" Josh dove in and swam fifty meters freestyle. When he tapped the side and popped his head up, he noticed a few other boys already getting out of the pool. He wasn't first. Not even second.

He looked up at the times and saw that he placed 5th.

"It's okay," he whispered to himself. "I can still make the team if I don't go below 5th in the rest of the races.

Next up was backstroke, in which he placed 4th. He then placed 5th in breaststroke. The final race was the butterfly. The one stroke he struggled with most.

As he stood ready to dive back into the pool for the final race in the tryout, he looked up and saw his family smiling and cheering for him. He gave them a thumbs up and dove in.

When he finished and looked up at his time, he saw that he placed 6th. He didn't make it. He didn't make the team. He hung his head, grabbed his towel, and ran to the changing rooms.

Dad, Mom, and Mia met him when he came out.

"I'm sorry, son. I know how important this tryout was for you," Dad said.

Mom gave him a big hug and they all walked out to the car together.

When they got home, Josh went up to his room and fell onto his bed facedown. Dad soon came in and sat down beside him.

"Did I ever tell you about the time I didn't make the baseball team?" Dad asked.

Josh looked up and shook his head. Dad went on to tell him about not making his hometown's baseball team. "I remember being filled with so many emotions. Anger at myself for not doing better. Disappointment at not making it. And even fear that I never would."

"Yeah," Josh muttered. "Me too."

"I remember Grandma coming into my room where I crashed on my bed, just like you did. She sat down with me and helped me pray to God about what I was feeling. I'd like to do that with you too," Dad said.

"What does God care about my swim tryout?" Josh asked.

"God cares about all your feelings. He made you to feel things. He wants you to tell Him about your feelings. Remember how David calls God his refuge in the book of Psalms? That's because God is our safe place. We come to Him with our feelings and ask for Him to help us."

"Even with failing to get on the swim team?" Josh asked.

Dad nodded.

"I'll try," Josh said. He sat up and bowed his head. He prayed and told God how he felt about not making the swim team. He admitted to feeling like a failure. He asked God to help him remember that he wasn't loved because of what he could do.

Dad also prayed for him and asked God to help Josh remember that he was God's child, and nothing could keep him from God's love. "You've created Josh for important work in your Kingdom. I pray you would prepare him for that work. I pray he would learn and grow from this experience. Help him to trust in your goodness to him," Dad prayed.

When they finished, Josh said, "Dad, even though this was really hard, I think I might want to try again. Maybe I'll get better with more practice. I don't want to give up."

Dad smiled. "Sounds like a plan. Remember that baseball team I told you about? I finally made the team on the third try."

Questions for Discussion

1. Have you ever tried hard to achieve something but failed at it? What did you feel?

2. Dad and Mom: share about a failure from your life and how you felt.

3. Read Psalm 18:1-2. Talk about the ways David describes God in this and in other Psalms: a rock, refuge, deliverer, shield, fortress. Why does he use these words?

4. Read Psalm 31:7, "I will rejoice and be glad in your steadfast love, because you have seen my affliction; you have known the distress of my soul." Tell your children that God sees their pain. He knows the cares of their heart. What does David say he will do in this verse?

5. While it is important to do our best at things, we aren't perfect, and sometimes we fail at things. We are finite creatures. Talk about this with your children. Talk about the one perfect person who ever lived: Jesus Christ. Talk about how through faith in who Christ is and what He did for us at the cross, God now looks at us and sees all the perfect things Jesus did.

6. Pray together, telling God how it feels when we fail at things. Ask Him for help in those failures. Thank Him for His love that never gives up on us. And thank Him for Jesus who was perfect for us.

Feeling Guilty

"Ok, guys, your mom said you had to finish your school work and clean your rooms before you play video games," Emma said, as she closed the front door behind Josh and Mia's parents.

Emma was a college student who sometimes watched Josh and Mia when their parents went out on a date. She attended their church and often helped teach their class in Sunday School. They liked when she came over because she always came up with fun things to do.

"After dinner, I have a new board game to try out. It requires a bit of acting. Who's up for practicing their thespian skills?" she asked.

"What's a thespian?" Mia asked from the dinner table, where she sat doing her math homework.

"Just a fancy word for actor," Emma explained.

"I don't like fancy words," Josh commented. "Simple is best." He groaned as he erased a wrong answer on his homework. "And I don't like worksheets!"

"Let me know if you need help," Emma said.

"I do," Josh admitted. Emma got in the chair beside him and started reading the instructions aloud. Mia got up and commented, "I'm going to clean my room now," and went upstairs.

A few minutes later, she came back down and sat on the couch. She picked up her tablet, put on her headset, and started playing a game.

Later, Emma, Josh, and Mia sat at the dinner table finishing up their pizza. Emma pointed to the board game box on the table and said, "Who's up for a game after we finish?"

Josh immediately said, "Me!"

Mia was silent.

"Mia?" Emma asked. "Are you okay?"

"Yeah. I think I'm going to pass on the game and just lie down in my room," she responded. Mia put her plate in the dishwasher and headed up to her room.

Emma soon followed and found her lying on her bed, staring up at the ceiling.

"What's happening?" she asked, taking a seat on the bean bag chair in the corner. From her spot on the bedroom floor, she spotted books and toys peaking out from under the bed.

Mia sighed. "Have you ever done something wrong and you just feel kind of yucky?" she asked Emma.

"Yes," Emma said. "What did you do wrong?"

Mia whispered, "I didn't do what you told us to do."

"Ah. You mean, like clean up your room before playing on your tablet?" she asked.

"Yes. I'm sorry, Emma. And I didn't finish my homework either." Mia felt herself start to cry.

Emma got up from the bean bag and came to sit beside Mia on the bed. "Mia, I know it doesn't feel like it right now, but that yucky feeling is really a good feeling. You are feeling guilt. It's your conscience telling you to repent. When we do something wrong, the Holy Spirit convicts us of sin so we would turn to God and repent of our sin."

"Really? It doesn't feel like a good thing at all," Mia responded.

"Do you remember how we've been talking about David in Sunday School?" Emma asked and Mia nodded. "Well, he sinned by taking a wife from one of his soldiers. He then felt guilty about it and he prayed to God and confessed his sin." She picked up Mia's Bible and read Psalm 51:1-2:

"Have mercy on me, O God,
according to your steadfast love;
according to your abundant mercy
blot out my transgressions.
Wash me thoroughly from my iniquity,
and cleanse me from my sin!"

"When we feel guilty because of something we did wrong, we need to pray and ask God for forgiveness and He forgives us because of what Jesus did for us at the cross," Emma said.

"Will you help me pray?" Mia asked.

"Of course," Emma said. Together, they prayed to God. Mia confessed for lying about cleaning her room and finishing her homework and asked for forgiveness.

"Amen," they said together.

Emma stood up. "So how about you finish your chores and school work and then we'll try out that new board game?" she said with a smile.

Mia nodded, and then smiled as she said, "I will on one condition: I can use props. You did say it was a game that involved acting ..."

Questions for Discussion

1. Have you ever felt "yucky" when you did something wrong?
Tell about that time.

2. Why would Emma tell Mia it was a good thing to feel that way?

3. Dad and Mom: share about a time you felt guilty for doing
something wrong.

4. Read Psalm 32:3-5. This is another psalm where David confesses sin.
How did David feel before he confessed his sin?
What happened when he prayed and confessed his sin?

5. For older kids, read the story about when Nathan confronted David for
his sin in 2 Samuel 12. How did David respond? (verse 13).
Talk with your children about how all our sin is against God.

6. Pray together, asking God for forgiveness for sin.
Rejoice and thank Him for providing forgiveness through Jesus Christ.

A Joy-Filled Heart

"It's finally here!" Mia announced as she came into the kitchen for breakfast.

"What's here?" Josh said, eating his bowl of cereal.

"The day I get to spend with Grandma," Mia responded. "And I better hurry, or I won't be ready when she comes to get me."

Mom came into the kitchen and asked, "Do you have everything you want to bring to Grandma's house?"

"Almost. I just need to pack up my paints. She said I could use some of her canvases. Is it okay if I bring our sprinkles from the pantry? We are going to bake cookies and I want to decorate them."

"Of course!" Mom said. "I look forward to hearing about your day when you get back tonight."

Mia heard the sound of a car door closing out front. "That's Grandma!" she announced and ran to the front door.

After Mia put her paints and other supplies in the car, she and Grandma drove off down the road. "First stop, is the botanical garden," Grandma announced.

"Really? I didn't know we were going there," Mia commented.

"I know. I thought we needed some inspiration before we start painting. We'll walk through the garden, take some photos, and then head home and set up in the studio," Grandma replied.

As they walked through the garden, Mia stopped every few steps to take a photo of a flower. "They are all so pretty!" she said. "I love those big cabbage roses the best."

"Wait until you see their collection of orchids," Grandma commented. "They are in the building over there," she pointed.

"That was amazing!" Mia said as she scrolled through the photos she took. "I've never seen a pitcher plant before. They look so strange. I think I may try painting them in the studio."

"God's creation is amazing," Grandma said. "Everything He has made tells us something about Him."

"I think pitcher plants tell us God has a sense of humor," Mia remarked.

They set up canvases in the studio and spent the afternoon painting the plants and flowers they saw at the garden.

Later, Mia and Grandma stood at the kitchen counter measuring ingredients for cookies. Mia turned to Grandma and said, "This has been the best day ever. I got to spend the day with you and do all my favorite things."

Grandma recited Psalm 118:24, "This is the day the Lord has made; let us rejoice and be glad in it."

Mia said, "We learned that verse in Sunday School."

Grandma turned off the mixer and turned to Mia. "Every day is a gift from the Lord. Whether it's a day filled with exciting things, like today, or a day that is filled with normal duties and activities. We praise the Lord for His goodness to us every day."

They finished putting the cookie dough onto the cookie sheets and placed them in the oven to cook. While they waited, Grandma sat with Mia and read to her from Psalm 145.

Grandma told Mia how the book of Psalms contains many different kinds of songs or poems that God's people sang in worship (and some churches still do so today). "Some songs are called the Psalms of Lament where the writer tells the Lord how sad or scared he feels and he asks God to help him," Grandma said.

"I know about those," Mia commented. "We've read some during family devotions."

Grandma continued, "Other Psalms call us to praise and rejoice in the goodness of God, for He has been so good to us."

"Like creating so many beautiful things," Mia remarked. "And giving us fun days like today."

"Yes," Grandma agreed. "And the very best thing is when He gave us His Son, Jesus, to die for us on the cross so we could be His children."

They heard the sound of the timer and got up to remove the cookies from the oven.

"How about as these cookies cool, we do some creative journaling together? Let's go through Psalm 145 and draw some of the things we learn about God from it," Grandma suggested.

"I think I'll draw some flowers, maybe some cabbage roses, and write out part of the Psalm," Mia said as she gathered up her art supplies.

Later, as they sat down to eat their cookies, Grandma and Mia prayed to God, praising Him for their day.

"Thank you for your goodness to us. Thank you for the gift of a fun day together. And thank you for my Grandma," Mia prayed.

"Should we save some cookies to bring home to your brother?" Grandma asked.

"Maybe ..." Mia said with a smile.

Questions for Discussion

1. Have you ever had a fun day like Mia did? A day where you did all the things you enjoy most? How did you feel?

2. Dad and Mom: share about a time when you felt the same.

3. Why should we stop and tell God about our joy at those times? Why should we praise Him each day? Talk about how all things are gifts from God, including the fun days we have. Those things are gifts for us to enjoy and to praise Him for.

4. For younger children, read a section of Psalm 145 and talk about some of the things God has done. How should we respond to what God has done?

5. For older children, read Psalm 145 together and make a list of all the things David says about God in this passage. How should we respond?

6. Pray together, praising God for His goodness. Praise Him for the joy He gives us in the good things He provides.

Who made this book?

Author: Christina Fox

Christina Fox is a counselor, retreat speaker, writer, and author of multiple books, including *Idols of a Mother's Heart* and *Tell God How You Feel*. She loves to help people see how the gospel intersects with their daily lives. You can find her at www.christinafox.com.

Illustrator: Lisa Flanagan

Lisa is an Australian illustrator of over twenty books for children, including *Tell God How You Feel* and the *God's Daring Dozen* series. She loves to create relatable characters that children connect with and enjoy.

CHRISTIAN FOCUS PUBLICATIONS

Christian Focus | Christian Heritage | CF4K | Mentor

Christian Focus Publications publishes books for adults and children under its four main imprints: Christian Focus, CF4K, Mentor and Christian Heritage. Our books reflect our conviction that God's Word is reliable and Jesus is the way to know him, and live for ever with him.

Our children's publication list covers pre-school to early teens. We also publish personal and family devotional titles, biographies and inspirational stories that children will love.

From pre-school board books to teenage apologetics, we have it covered!

Christian Focus Publications Ltd,
Geanies House, Fearn, Ross-shire,
IV20 1TW, Scotland,
United Kingdom.

Find us at our web page: www.christianfocus.com

CF4•K
Because you're never too young to know Jesus